MW01504284

I Serve You The Back of Jesus

Look At the Back of Jesus

Lois François

WESTBOW
PRESS®
A DIVISION OF THOMAS NELSON
& ZONDERVAN

Copyright © 2015 Lois François.

All rights reserved. No part of this book may be used or reproduced by any means, graphic, electronic, or mechanical, including photocopying, recording, taping or by any information storage retrieval system without the written permission of the author except in the case of brief quotations embodied in critical articles and reviews.

Cover image by Jillian Allen

This book is a work of non-fiction. Unless otherwise noted, the author and the publisher make no explicit guarantees as to the accuracy of the information contained in this book and in some cases, names of people and places have been altered to protect their privacy.

Scripture taken from the King James Version of the Bible.

Scripture taken from the *Amplified Bible*, copyright © 1954, 1958, 1962, 1964, 1965, 1987 by The Lockman Foundation. Used by permission.

WestBow Press books may be ordered through booksellers or by contacting:

WestBow Press
A Division of Thomas Nelson & Zondervan
1663 Liberty Drive
Bloomington, IN 47403
www.westbowpress.com
1 (866) 928-1240

Because of the dynamic nature of the Internet, any web addresses or links contained in this book may have changed since publication and may no longer be valid. The views expressed in this work are solely those of the author and do not necessarily reflect the views of the publisher, and the publisher hereby disclaims any responsibility for them.

Any people depicted in stock imagery provided by Thinkstock are models, and such images are being used for illustrative purposes only. Certain stock imagery © Thinkstock.

ISBN: 978-1-5127-1317-6 (sc)
ISBN: 978-1-5127-1318-3 (hc)
ISBN: 978-1-5127-1319-0 (e)

Library of Congress Control Number: 2015915391

Print information available on the last page.

WestBow Press rev. date: 09/23/2015

Contents

I would like to dedicate this book to my wonderful sister, Yvonne Heath-Retemeyer Williams, who willingly obeyed the voice of God, always placing her needs aside to be of service to my family. Known to my children as *Aunt Blessed*, Yvonne took on the role of a second mother to them. They often referred to her as a nurturing and giving aunt who was always amusing and joyful. She ministered to my children in every area of their lives, instilling lifelong values—values that have helped mold them into the God-fearing individuals they are today. Presently, she is with the Lord but will always be remembered for her unselfishness, unconditional love, and generosity. She was truly a mighty woman of God, and for this, we give God thanks.

Foreword

When I was first asked to write about my mother, I was nervous and anxious. As an outspoken young lady who would normally love to write and reflect on her life, I worried about this task. I did not know if I was ready to show this latent side of me, this sensitive and uncontrolled, emotional side that has been so carefully constructed to display this so-called me. There are many layers that I have so meticulously molded and redefined in order to suppress the true me, for I am my mother's daughter, and all that she experiences, all that she lives, flows through me.

When I was growing up, only a few (family, friends, and church family) knew the struggles my mother was facing. Yet even then, the only true spectators were us, her immediate family. My father, the head of the household, was rarely at home, because his two jobs occupied most of his time. However, when he was home, he was taking care of my little sister, brothers, and me and maintaining the house while also looking after my mother. I do not think as a child that my mother's true condition dawned on me. I just knew she was always in bed, unable to hold my little sister, braid my hair, or even read good-night stories to us.

As the years passed, I began to see my mom battle with lupus and rheumatoid arthritis. However, it was not until I was older, as my mother shared her stories, that pieces of my life began to connect; events started to coincide and make sense. I always knew my mother was sick but never really grasped what we as a family went through, or at least I thought I did not. What I failed to realize was that though my mother was a strong woman (endurance-wise), the pain and heartache she went through formed emotional voids and challenges in my life: having to constantly worry about whether or not your mother was going to fall down and die that day; contemplating how you were going to explain to your little sister that though she had a mother who loved her, her mom was called to a better place; tearing up at the thought of your father as a widower struggling not only with the loss of his wife but also with raising his four children; or just hoping that you did not become an individual who went through life with an unspoken void, seeking to fill that emptiness at any cost due to the lack of experiencing true maternal love. Thoughts like these and more would surface in my mind as I observed my mother's condition.

What would confuse me, however, was how throughout her pain she would persist in saying she was healed. I do believe in faith and the power of the tongue, but I felt that her outlook was irritatingly impractical and overly optimistic. She would always speak of the importance of confessions and walking in God's obedience—how death and life are controlled by what you say. I understand that, I truly do, but how could one who has suffered from pain and agony for many years still continue to say she is healed?

As soon as her health would get better, the Devil would attack her again. She would get a new job and then have to take time off in order to regain strength and better health. If she was not experiencing a crucial illness, then she would be dealing with the daily pains of arthritis. This made me give up on my mom and her confessions. My doubt was so strong that I would sometimes wish she would just die so she would not have to go through such pain—so I would not have to constantly worry about whether I was going to be motherless the next day.

I remember having an intense confrontation in which I scolded her: "Mom, why don't you just stop working? It is not for you. You work, and then get sick and have to go to the hospital, get better, and start working again, and the cycle continues. Just stop working!" How could someone who was healed have to always deal with pain? Not a week would go by without my mom expressing her feelings of dizziness, nausea, or back and joint pains. I was just tired of it all. There had to be more to life than this hurt I was used to seeing, these wounds I was feeling, and this oppression my mother was fighting. Even as I relayed all of this to my mom, she simply said, "Lorissa, I will stop working due to choice, not due to any sickness that the Devil is trying to bring upon me to destroy my body. He has no control over my body and my ability to work; God does."

Even this startled me. Nevertheless, through all of this, there is a God—a loving God who heals and restores the unhealthy and the broken, who comforts the hurting, and who delights Himself in His children. If there is one thing I have learned from my mother, it is the importance of standing on the Word of God. Now,

I do not mean literally taking a Bible and standing on it but rather living and speaking the Scriptures.

I am confident in saying that my mom would not be alive and healthy today if it had not been for her strong and consistent faith in God and His Word. Regardless of the situation, my mom knew that sickness was not an option. She would always quote healing Scriptures and would stay prayed up. She knew that the easiest way to fall victim to the Enemy's attacks is by leaving yourself spiritually empty and therefore vulnerable.

Even I was able to experience this. While helping my mother edit this book, the Devil tried to attack me. One night while sleeping, I felt a dark, demonic spirit try to come and take my breath away. Shocked, I started pleading the blood of Jesus over myself as my mom has always done. "Satan, the blood of Jesus is against you! I plead the blood of Jesus over me. Take your hands off me!" The more I declared these words, the less control this spirit had, and eventually it went away. As I awoke the next morning, I was in awe. The Devil had tried to attack me during my time of ministry. Nevertheless, by God's grace I was able to heed to my mother's example and stand firm on the Word of God. My mother's witness actually became a reality for me.

Through my mom's testimony I have been able to truly understand who God is and what He has done for me. I now realize why there was such a deep sense of hurt that plagued my heart for many years. I was so used to being the older sister who helped out and who focused on the needs of others before myself that I did not realize how much love I was missing—the love of the Father. I was so accustomed to seeing pain that I was oblivious to the joy Jesus brings. Now all these emotions and blurred layers are no longer concealed. Yes, it is hard, but as I continue to be transparent with God, my parents, and myself, God has begun to reveal to me things in the spiritual and physical realm. He reminds me of His promises in His Word: "But ye are a chosen generation, a royal priesthood, an holy nation, a peculiar people; that ye should shew forth the praises of him who hath called you out of darkness into his marvelous light." (1 Peter 2:9 KJV) I am thrilled to see what else the Lord has in store for me, my family, and those He places on our hearts to minister to.

This book, *I Serve You the Back of Jesus*, shows you the story of a praying mother—a woman who, though she dealt with several life-threatening illnesses, remained faithful to God and allowed Him to use her mightily; a strong and mighty woman of God who is a powerhouse full of love, hope, and faith. May my mother's testimony be the seed that is sown into your life—a seed that will cultivate God's love and abundant grace into your daily walk with Christ.

—Lorissa Francois, age eighteen,
eldest daughter of Lois Francois

Preface

On Wednesday, February 6, 2013, while praying and fasting, the Lord reminded me of the book He told me to write years ago regarding my fight with lupus and rheumatoid arthritis, and my healing. This was then followed by clear instructions on its title. In obedience, I present to you, *I Serve You the Back of Jesus*.

Acknowledgments

Special thanks go to the following people:

To my pastors, Randy and Cherie Gilbert, of Faith Landmarks Ministries in Richmond, Virginia, for being my spiritual leaders and for always having a timely word. Thank you for equipping me on how to effectively use the Word of God.

To my editor and loving daughter, Lorissa Francois, who set aside time from her busy school and work schedule to assist me in this endeavor.

To my friend and coeditor, Catherine Elcock, who in spite of her demanding schedule also sacrificed time to help edit this book.

To my beloved husband, Nero, who worked tirelessly throughout the years of my fight with lupus to meet the needs of our family. Thanks, honey, for your love, patience, and support!

To the wonderful gifts God has blessed my husband and me with: Shane, Joel, Lorissa, and Lo-Ann, who never complained even when the going got tough but kept praying and doing their best.

To my brother, Joseph Norton, and sisters, Naomi Williams and Eunice Alleyne, for all the help they have given to my family.

To my sister, Glennis Smith, and the wonderful women of the Brooklyn Tabernacle Church Prayer Brand: Winnifred Pearson, Sharon Smith, Natalie Williams, and Braveney Ghullike.

To my friend Karen Williams for allowing God to use her significantly in my healing.

To a true and special friend, Denyse Charles, who faithfully took care of my children for years, refusing any monetary compensation.

To all of my siblings and friends who encouraged and prayed me through my physical discomfort.

Last I would like to thank my wonderful parents, the late Pastor Harry Norton and Louise Norton, who have been towers of strength during my fight with lupus. Through the teachings of the Word of God and through their daily lifestyle, they instilled in me as a child the importance and power of faith-based prayer. My father's life was an encouraging testimony of the awesome power of God, and my mother continues to be the praying powerhouse of our family. Thanks, Mom, for all your prayers and encouraging words and for being a woman of the Word. May God's presence continue to encompass you as His blessings overtake you.

Chapter

I Serve You the Back of Jesus

As I stepped out of bed, I stood there bent over, motionless, and in shock by an intense pain that suddenly attacked my back. Paralyzed by this excruciating, unbearable blow, I cried out, "My God, what is this!"

I had been painless for years, and this feeling, so savagely violent in nature, could not have been a simple coincidence. This pain was similar to whiplash, which I had formerly experienced. Within an instant, several feet away from my bed but in front of me, a human figure appeared in a vision. Short in stature, wrinkled, and old, this man stood staring at me with a hard and brutal look. Bent over with a humped back, this big-headed man was dressed in a khaki shirt and shorts. As he tried to step closer to my bed, immediately Jesus appeared with his beaten and blood-striped back facing me.

Almost automatically, I heard myself saying, "I serve you the back of Jesus! Look at the back of Jesus! I serve you the back of Jesus! Look at the back of Jesus!"

As I declared these words repeatedly, the wretched man turned away in fear. Trembling, he walked away, never looking at the blood-stained back of Jesus. As he slowly disappeared, with every step he took, the pain in my back lessened. When he finally vanished, and following the departure of Jesus, the pain completely left my body, allowing me to stand erect.

I rubbed my eyes in astonishment, and I knew I was not dreaming; I was wide awake. A few minutes later when I went to the bathroom to get ready for work, I asked my heavenly Father, "God, what was that?"

He answered, "My daughter, I have opened your eyes for a moment so you can see what is occurring in the spiritual realm. I healed you, but the Enemy came back to bring sickness upon you. That was a crippling demon that attacked you, and if you had only gone back to bed, saying, *I am sick and cannot work today*, that crippling spirit would have taken over your body and condemned you. I opened your eyes for you so you could see that the pain you felt was unnatural, so you will not quit but fight. It was the Enemy attacking your body, trying to condemn you to your bed permanently."

In amazement and somewhat speechless, I uttered, "My God, my God, my God. Thank You."

As I reflected on this incident, I recalled my pastor's sermons that would often remind us of the importance of the stripes Jesus took on His back for us two thousand years ago. Though we are healed, the Enemy tries to come back and bring symptoms of sickness to our bodies. Therefore, we must decide whether or not we want to receive the healing that is given to us through Jesus or if we are going to accept the symptoms the Devil is trying to place upon us. Therefore, it is very important that we confess only the Word of God at all times, regardless of how we feel or what we see, so we can claim and receive this healing. As I meditated on this and the words of my heavenly Father, I spent the rest of my day in prayer and praise, thanking God for His healing power and unfailing love.

Surely he hath borne our griefs, and carried our sorrows; yet we did esteem him stricken, smitten of God, and afflicted. But he was wounded for our transgressions, he was bruised for our iniquities: the chastisement of our peace was upon him; and with his stripes we are healed. (Isa. 53. 4–5 KJV)

Surely He has borne our griefs (sicknesses, weaknesses, and distresses) and carried our sorrows and pains [of punishment], yet we [ignorantly] considered Him stricken, smitten, and afflicted by God [as if with leprosy]. But He was wounded for our transgressions, He was bruised for our guilt and iniquities; the chastisement [needful to obtain] peace and well-being for us was upon Him, and with the stripes [that wounded] Him we are healed and made whole. (Isa. 53:4–5 AMP)

Chapter

What's Next?

This demonic encounter took place about three years after the Lord healed me of lupus and rheumatoid arthritis. My six-year fight with lupus all began in Brooklyn, New York, where I resided at the time. One Saturday afternoon my husband was driving our family, and we were waiting at a traffic light. A car overtaking a bus at a high speed came from the opposite direction. The driver lost control and ran into our car. Though none of our children were injured, unfortunately I immediately experienced severe neck and back pain. After being seen by a doctor, I was told that I was suffering from the effects of whiplash. I endured several months of therapy, only for my condition to get better and then get worse as the pain began to develop in other parts of my body. My doctor conducted many tests and said I had premature arthritis.

Ignorantly I asked, "Arthritis—is that not a condition for the elderly?"

To my surprise, I was told that even babies can fall susceptible to this illness. I was treated for this condition, but in a few weeks my entire body was afflicted with intense pain. This pain felt as if it took over 90 percent of my body, and the medications that once worked had lost their effectiveness. My doctor recognized that there was something else occurring in my body. He said he was going to send me to another hospital, where I would obtain fast service and attention. He also suggested that more tests should be done in order to find out what had caused the drastic increase of pain.

Upon my arrival at the recommended hospital, I got the best care and attention one could desire. Many tests were done, and I was informed that the added pain was due to a condition called lupus. When I received this news, though I was surprised, I smiled.

Following my reaction to his diagnosis, the doctor sternly looked at me and asked, "Do you know what lupus is?"

"Yes," I replied, "I have an idea."

I smiled because as soon as I got the report from the doctor, the Lord said to me, "Whose report will you believe?" Having heard these words, I gained strength and confidence in knowing that my God, *Jehovah Rapha*, is the ultimate healer. The doctor then went into a detailed explanation of the disease and gave me a plan of treatment. He sent me home with medications and follow-up appointments.

As if the news could not get any worse, the following week I had an eye appointment that had to be done before I could use one of the medications. At the completion of the eye examination, I was told that I had glaucoma in both eyes and needed surgery as soon as possible. My condition was very serious and could lead to blindness at any given moment. After much prayer, I went ahead and agreed to complete the surgery.

Later that week, I got another negative report about an infection resulting in more pain and stress to my body. This was followed by frequent medical appointments and the implementation of additional medications. The months went by, and the deterioration of my body was evident as I began to rapidly lose weight. I was told that my blood was clotting, and though I was given some medication, there was no improvement.

While I was visiting my doctor and inquiring about my blood, she bluntly stated, "Your blood is not going to get better."

That day I left the hospital angry—angry at the Devil and at the words of my doctor. When I got home, I got on my knees before the Lord and said, "God, You heard what the doctor said, and now You will prove her wrong. My blood will return to the way it should be— the way you made it."

I went into prayer and fasting for seven days, abstaining from all of my medication. I would not recommend this to anyone, but I wanted God to prove the doctor wrong. Some family members were surprised that I decided to fast in the condition I was in. One even asked me if I thought that was a wise thing to do, but I felt confident in my God. I was desperate for His help, and I knew He would come through for me. I wanted God to get all the credit when the results from my blood test after the fast returned to normal.

After my fast, another blood test was taken, and a week, later I met with my doctor to discuss the results. She looked at the results from the tests, turned back to the notes from the previous visits, and then turned back again to the results. She did this about three times.

In response to her perplexed look and because of my impatience, I interrupted her. Anxiously I asked, "What are the results of the blood work?"

In a very soft and unbelieving voice, she said, "Your blood is normal. There are no signs of blood clots."

I shouted, *"Thank You, Jesus!* You did it! That is the power of prayer; God did it!"

She said nothing. However, I left there rejoicing, remembering the words my Father said to me on the day I was told I had lupus: "Whose report will you believe?" Just as God removed the clotting from my blood, I was confident that He will one day heal me entirely from lupus.

> Bless the Lord, O my soul: and forget not all his benefits: Who forgiveth all thine iniquities: who healeth all thy diseases: Who redeemeth thy life from destruction; and crowneth thee with loving kindness and tender mercies; Who satisfieth thy mouth with good things; so that thy youth is renewed like the eagle's. (Ps. 103:2–5 KJV)

> Bless (affectionately, gratefully praise) the Lord, O my soul, and forget not [one of]

all His benefits—Who forgives [every one of] all your iniquities, Who heals [each one of] all your diseases, Who redeems your life from the pit and corruption, Who beautifies, dignifies, and crowns you with loving-kindness and tender mercy; Who satisfies your mouth [your necessity and desire at your personal age and situation] with good so that your youth, renewed, is like the eagle's [strong, overcoming, soaring]! (Ps. 103:2–5 AMP)

Chapter

3

God Chuckled

It was another day home with the children. I was at the kitchen sink washing dishes when suddenly I experienced severe weakness and lightheadedness. This attack was followed by a headache and intense pain throughout my entire body. Though I began pleading the blood of Jesus over my body, the feeling got worse to the point where I felt as though I was about to collapse.

I continued declaring the blood of Jesus over my body and slowly walked into the living room, where my children were playing. As soon as I went to the sofa to lie down, my two-year-old daughter stopped playing and walked over to a jar of Vaseline petroleum jelly that was on the table. She reached in, took some out, and walked over to her older siblings, who were playing. She then placed some petroleum jelly on each of their foreheads, saying, "Blood Jesus, blood Jesus, blood Jesus." She also placed some on her forehead, repeating the same words: "Blood Jesus, blood Jesus." At this time her brothers and sister were laughing at her, but my two-year-old was very serious. She was on a mission and allowed nothing or no one to distract or stop her.

After anointing herself, she came over to me; she anointed my forehead with the petroleum jelly and said, "Blood Jesus, blood Jesus, blood Jesus." With boldness, power, and a stern look on her face, she then marched around the room. With her fist in the air and in a warlike manner, she started repeating those powerful words again: "Blood Jesus, blood Jesus, blood Jesus!" Then she began speaking in tongues. Now, you may be a bit skeptical about a two-year-old speaking in tongues, but I knew what I heard. Immediately the atmosphere in the room changed. The power of God was present; there was such an anointing in the room that instantly the pain, dizziness, and lightheadedness left my body. After my little Lo-Ann completed her warfare and sent that spirit of sickness away, she went back to playing as normal, like nothing ever happened.

In excitement and amazement I exclaimed, "My God, my God, my God! How awesome You are. Thank You, Jesus!"

I then heard a chuckle—yes, a chuckle—followed by a laugh. My God had laughed, and so I began laughing too. We laughed and laughed and laughed; we had a good time.

The Lord then said to me, "The Enemy tried to take you down to the point where you could not even get to the phone to call someone to pray for you or help you, but little did he know help was right there in your house. I chose to use your two-year-old, the youngest of your four children, to remind him of who I am and the power I possess. I can use a two-year-old; I can flow through a little child to heal you of this dizziness and pain."

I was in awe at what had just occurred. It was not that I did not know the power of God, but the way in which He used my two-year-old daughter was amazing; her intense focus on her mission at hand was astonishing. That was nothing but the power of God operating in my daughter's life. God is indeed an awesome God.

Having lost the pain and overcome that awful sick feeling, I jumped to my feet and burst out in laughter and praise. My heavenly Father and I laughed together. I then sang and danced before the Lord for some time and basked in His wonderful presence. Being in His presence was so sweet that I did not want to leave; I called it my *sweet victory.*

At the end of this sweet fellowship, I asked my Father, "Why did Lo-Ann use Vaseline?"

He responded, "Lo-Ann was accustomed to seeing you anoint her and her siblings with olive oil, laying your hands on their foreheads, and praying. The olive oil was not in her reach, so I directed her to the Vaseline, which was within her reach. I also directed her to cover her siblings and herself before laying hands on you."

Every time I mention or recount this incident, I feel such a strong anointing, and I am always amazed at the awesomeness of God. It was as if God was telling the Devil, "I am going to use a little child—a two-year-old—to put you in your place." The day continued, and I was able to accomplish all of my tasks pain-free. *To God be the glory!*

> I will sing unto the Lord, for he hath triumphed gloriously: the horse and his rider hath he thrown into the sea. The Lord is my strength and song, and he has become my salvation;...The Lord is a man of war: the Lord is his name. ... Thy right

hand, O Lord, is become glorious in power: Thy right hand, O Lord, hath dashed in pieces the enemy. (Exod. 15:1–3, 6 KJV)

Then Moses and the Israelites sang this song to the Lord, saying, I will sing to the Lord, for He has triumphed gloriously; the horse and his rider or its chariot has He thrown into the sea. The Lord is my Strength and my Song, and He has become my Salvation; this is my God, and I will praise Him, my father's God, and I will exalt Him. The Lord is a Man of War; the Lord is His name. ... Your right hand, O Lord, is glorious in power; Your right hand, O Lord, shatters the enemy. (Exod. 15:1–3, 6 AMP)

Chapter

Whose Report Will You Believe?

It is ironic how the moment we begin to boast about the goodness of God and His miraculous power, we find ourselves under attack, plagued by the Devil's retaliation. Some months after this miraculous act of God through my daughter, the Devil was enraged. Pain increased in my hands and feet, and there was an increase of severe weakness in my joints. Due to the intensity of the pain, I had to quit my job as an assistant kindergarten teacher and stay at home, where all of my time was spent in bed. It worsened to the point that if I needed to use the bathroom, I would have to wait for my husband to help me. When he was at work and no one was there to help me, I would roll out of the bed and crawl to the bathroom, which was many feet away, oftentimes not making it there in time.

It was during these vulnerable times that I remembered the words God said to me when I first got the diagnosis: "Whose report will you believe?" With tears in my eyes I would confess the Word, "By His stripes I am healed" (Isa. 53:5 KJV), "I can do all things through Christ who strengthens me" (Phil. 4:13 KJV), and other Scripture verses the Lord brought to mind. It was very painful, but I commanded my body (in the name of Jesus) to do what I needed to do. I stood on those words day and night, along with other Scriptures on healing.

After several months of illness, my husband had to get another job to help take care of the bills. He would take our kindergartner to school and my two-year-old to her babysitter and then go to work. He would bring them home in the evening and then return to work, many times coming home at one or two o'clock in the morning from his second job. He would then get up at six thirty to get the girls ready for school and the sitter.

My boys, who were six and nine at the time, helped themselves and walked to and from school. Shane my nine-year-old, would willingly offer to braid one of his sister's hair while my husband would braid the other.

Shane, being observant, noticed that his dad had to work very hard and his mother was sick in bed, unable to do anything, so he started cleaning the bathroom, washing dishes, and doing whatever he could put his hand to do. Even when I would say it was too much for him to do, he insisted that he could do it and always did it willingly with a smile.

Joel, my six-year-old, ever singing and smiling, would bring me wildflowers that he picked on his way home from school or while he was outside playing. I can remember him expressing how much he missed when I would take him and his siblings to the park every evening, Monday through Friday, to play basketball. Joel would not leave the park until he got the ball in the hoop. (This often resulted in me having to lift him up in order for him to shoot the ball.) He would often pray, "Dear God, please heal my mom so we can play basketball." He never got tired of praying, even when he did not see any improvements. He continued to pray and believe that God would heal his mother.

At the end of that school year when I looked at my kindergartner's report card, I was saddened when I read that she was tardy almost every day. However, I took comfort in knowing that God knew I could not help and that my husband was doing his best. On the other hand, I was delighted to see that she was excelling both academically and behaviorally. With no help from her mom and minimal assistance from her dad, she achieved an excellent report card; I knew it was due to no one but God. My boys also got excellent report cards, and again I was convinced that it was all God's doing. Despite all the stress and all that was lacking in their lives, they did it. They were more than conquerors, as God was surely there for them. To God be the glory because *great* things He has done!

I spent many days lying in bed with my Bible on my chest. Though I read the Word and prayed, I would often feel incomplete because I felt I needed to do more but was physically restrained. Then one day I received a phone call from a sister at church requesting prayer for her husband and children. A few days later, other women began calling for prayer for their husbands and children as well. Now, some people would not understand why I would begin to pray for other families' situations when I was struggling with lupus and arthritis. However, now I had something to do, a purpose; I started interceding for families. I allowed the Lord to use me even as I was dealing with my own sicknesses. At nights when I could not sleep due to pain, the Lord would bring names of people to me, mainly husbands and wives, for me to intercede on their behalf. He sometimes showed me the faces of people I did not know. I would then pray for them as the Holy Spirit led me. This began my ministry of intercession.

As I looked around my house some months later and saw all that needed to be done, I became very sad, as I knew I could not physically do anything for my children. My heart was saddened at the thought of not being able to hold or play with my youngest child, who was only six months old when I initially became ill. I felt as though I did not bond with her as I was able to with my other children. I reflected on all the things she was missing at that tender age, and I felt useless. You see, I thought that by now I would have gotten better and would have been of some use to my family, but I was not.

As a result of the increased pain in my body, I was very weak. My husband now had to lift me from my bed to take me wherever I needed to go. It was very painful to be incompetent to my family. So one day I asked the Lord, "Lord, why am I still here? I am of no use to my family. Why don't You take me home?"

My Father then said to me in a sweet, gentle voice, "You are not useless to your family! Right now the Enemy is mad at you. Do not underestimate the power of your prayers for your family and others. You are breaking strongholds in the lives of people on your sick bed. In your pain I am using you."

I repented and asked the Lord for strength and that I would not look at things naturally but would remember that He was working in the spiritual realm on my behalf. I began thanking Him for His daily provision, for the protection of my husband and children, and for helping them to focus at school.

As time went by, there were some good days and some not-so-good days. There is a saying that states, "The Devil only messes with you when he knows you are a threat to him." Well, that was the case with me; he tried to discourage me once more by an escalation of pain in my body. I recall at one time there was a period where I could not use my hands. They were so painful and swollen that I could not even hold a pen or my toothbrush, but I kept confessing God's Word over my body. The healing Scriptures were constantly on my lips and after a while I saw a decrease in swelling and pain.

On another occasion, I would wake up with stiff, painful fingers, some of them turned inward toward the palm of my hands. They were tightly and painfully balled. Though I tried to straighten them, they would not move. I remembered hearing the Devil's voice: "You will be crippled; your fingers will not straighten."

Rebuking that voice, I would pour anointing oil on my hands, saying, "Fingers, you will straighten in the name of Jesus, and you will remain straight the way God made you." I would painfully extend my fingers while speaking the Word of God over them persistently. They would eventually straighten out and feel fine for the rest of the day.

However, as I would go to sleep and wake up, I would be in the same crippling predicament. After this happened for the third time, an anger toward the Devil arose, and I said to him, "Satan, you will no longer mess with my body. In the name of Jesus, thou crippling spirit, loose my fingers! By the stripes of Jesus I am whole. Fingers, you will straighten out and not turn inward anymore." And that was the end of that. My fingers never turned inward again.

Previous to this, my sister informed me of a young lady at her church who had been sick with lupus for some time. She shared with her the many struggles she was facing and made sure to emphasize that I, Lois, had *many more things to go through*. This was then followed by a list of phases that I should expect and a book that would help me cope with these stages. Some days later my sister brought the book and gave it to me. Uninterested, I refused to read or even touch that book.

I was determined to be healed and therefore would not accept the possibility of experiencing any more *stages*.

A week later my mother came to visit me and saw the book. As an avid reader, she was always looking for a good read, so she began reading. However, before she was halfway through the book, my mother came to me in tears. "My God, have mercy," she said. "This is a terrible disease. My daughter, I am so glad you decided not to read this book. You made a wise choice."

The book was filled with depictions of lupus's phases. It was so gruesome that it would cause one to lose all faith. It also gave a vivid description of a teacher who had lupus and how she suffered through every phase of it. I said to my mother, "I will believe only the report of the Lord. His report says I am healed. Therefore I am healed, and I will only feed my spirit on the Word of God."

This sister in the Lord who had lupus thought she was helping me by preparing me for the worst. Unfortunately, she did not know better. The Word of God says, "My people perish for a lack of knowledge" (Hosea 4:6). I thank God that I knew Him and I knew who I was in Christ. No matter what this disease was supposed to entail, I knew Jesus took the stripes on His back for my healing. I also knew that what I meditated on and allowed to get into my spirit, whether it was through reading, listening to, or confessing, would eventually become a part of my being. Knowing God's Word is a blessing, as it is power and life and surpasses all medical diagnoses.

> I love thee, O Lord, my strength. The Lord is my rock, and my fortress, and my deliverer; my God, my strength, in whom I will trust; my buckler, and the horn of my salvation, and my high tower. I will call unto the Lord, who is worthy to be praised: so shall I be saved from mine enemies. ... It is God that girdeth me with strength, and maketh my way perfect. (Ps. 18:1–3, 32 KJV)

> I love You fervently and devotedly, O Lord, my Strength. The Lord is my Rock, my Fortress, and my Deliverer; my God, my keen and firm Strength in Whom I will trust and take refuge, my Shield, and the Horn of my salvation, my High Tower. I will call upon the Lord, Who is to be praised; so shall I be saved from my enemies. ... The God who girds me with strength and makes my way perfect. (Ps. 18:1–3, 32 AMP)

Chapter

He Is an on-Time God, and His Ways Are Past Finding Out!

It is not only important to know God's Word, but one must also realize that God's doings are not done within our time but in His time. As stated in Psalm 27:14, we are to wait on the Lord, be strong, and let our hearts take courage.

As I reflect on this verse, I am reminded of a time when God proved Himself by rewarding me for trusting in Him. Surprisingly, one day my sister, Glennis, came to visit me with some of her prayer band ladies from the Brooklyn Tabernacle Church in Brooklyn, New York. They not only prayed but shared the Word of God with me while joyfully cleaning my house, laundering my family's clothes, and cooking some delicious meals. They did it all with the sweet love of God, filling my home with such a sweet aroma. After they left my house, I was not only spiritually uplifted but physically as well.

The following day I was even more surprised when one of the sisters came back to cook more delicious dishes for me and my family. I was blown away by such love. She came all the way from the Bronx to my house in Queens, riding the train and bus in the cold, to bless my family. A woman I did not know and who I had just met the previous day traveled great lengths to bless me. She even bought the food items she used to prepare the meals with her own money. That is what I call God's love in action. *To God be all the praise, honor, and glory.*

I often thank God for these wonderful ladies who made themselves available to minister to me and my family with such love and kindness at a time of great need. This was God answering an unuttered prayer. He knew it was my desire to have my house thoroughly cleaned but that I was restrained because of the sickness. So He worked it out; He sent the people with the right heart and spirit at the right time to fill that need. Is God not awesome? Not only is He awesome but He is also an on-time God—always on time with just what we need!

Another instance of God's perfect timing was shown through the kindness of my sister, Naomi. A few months after I was diagnosed with lupus, Naomi, who was going on a vacation overseas with her two children, offered to take my four children with her. Upon seeing my struggle with pain, she lovingly suggested that this time of separation would allow me to get some rest and take care of myself. I was happy for the help but was concerned about her traveling with and caring for six children, ages eighteen months to nine years old. She assured me that she could manage and that everything would be fine. I just needed to rest, care for myself, and get better.

As we proceeded to get my children ready for the trip, we were informed that obtaining a passport took six to eight weeks. Now, this was a problem, due to the fact that my sister was scheduled to travel in three weeks. My brother, Simeon, who was visiting from St. Vincent, heard of our ordeal and willingly offered to drive us from New York to Washington, DC, to the passport office to get the passports expedited. We received the passports by mail the following day.

I remembered being very exhausted after the trip but was thankful to God for showing up at the right time with the help I needed. I needed to rest as the doctor prescribed, and God sent my sister Naomi to help. I needed to get the passports expedited, and God used my brother, Simeon, to help in that area. I cannot begin to thank Him enough for His unfailing love. Because of His love for us, He goes beyond our expectations to meet our needs. Thank God my children were able to go on a vacation, away from an atmosphere of sickness and pain. They had a great time seeing a new place, meeting new people, and enjoying another culture.

Some weeks later, a dear friend of mine named Karen who had just lost her husband to cancer gave me hundreds of dollars to be treated by a holistic doctor. I refused to take the money, saying to her, "I should be giving you money seeing you have just lost your husband and have three children to care for."

My dear friend insisted that I take the money, saying, "Lois, this is not from me, it is from the Lord; take it."

I gratefully took it from her, thanking her for her sacrificial gift and thanking God for His provision. This kind, loving act from an unexpected source brought me to tears to see yet another sister in Christ unselfishly giving. At her time of loss and need, she had the right to look out for herself and children, but she saw my need, and out of love and compassion, she chose to bless me.

In addition to Karen, God used another friend to bless me. After visiting the doctor, I was prescribed some natural cleansers and builders, which cost hundreds of dollars. This dear friend gave me the money to take care of the prescription.

Here are two women of God who, in spite of their present need, chose to bless me. I never approached them and asked for help. However, because they heeded the voice of God, they saw my need and acted accordingly. I know that their sacrificial and unselfish act of giving was honored by God.

> But my God shall supply all your need according to his riches in glory by Christ Jesus. (Phil. 4:19 KJV)

> And my God will liberally supply ([a]fill to the full) your every need according to His riches in glory in Christ Jesus. (Phil. 4:19 AMP)

Chapter

Don't Mess with My Property

Just as the Devil persists in antagonizing God's children, we are also to be persistent in rebuking him. The Devil must be reminded about who we are and whose we are.

One morning I was awakened at 2:00 with unbearable pain. I sensed a strange presence in my room and heard a voice saying, "You will die. You will die." Immediately I rebuked that voice and confessed the Word of God over my life. After several hours of confession, the pain eased and I was able to go back to sleep. This same incident occurred the next two mornings.

On this third morning, however, at the sound of this tormenting voice, I felt another presence in my room. This presence was closer, stronger, and more powerful.

It was my Father—*the great I Am, the omnipotent One, the Lion of the tribe if Judah!* Within seconds, I found myself standing on my feet, and with boldness and power I heard myself saying, "I shall not die, but live, and declare the works of the Lord, and I will live to see my children's children's, children" (Ps. 118:17 KJV). I then continued to confess the Word of God.

Immediately, that spirit of death left my room, and I basked in the sweet presence of my God, praising and thanking Him for His healing power. That was when I looked at myself because I was in shock. I was standing on my own two feet, and it felt good. God came into my room, lifted me up, and placed me on my feet. As I mentioned previously, I could not walk on my own, so I knew that this was nothing but God's mighty hand. The God who shut the mouth of the lion when Daniel was in the lion's den is the same God who shut the mouth of the Enemy when he tried to speak death into my life. He is the same yesterday, today, and forever. *Glory to His name!*

Who can stand before his indignation? and who can abide in the fierceness of his anger? his fury is poured out like fire, and the rocks are thrown down by him. The

Lord is good, a strong hold in the day of trouble; and he knoweth them that trust in him. (Nah. 1:6–7 KJV)

Who can stand before His indignation? And who can stand up and endure the fierceness of His anger? His wrath is poured out like fire, and the rocks are broken asunder by Him. The Lord is good, a Strength and Stronghold in the day of trouble; He knows (recognizes, has knowledge of, and understands) those who take refuge and trust in Him. (Nah. 1:6–7 AMP)

For by thee I have run through a troop; and by my God have I leaped over a wall. As for God, his way is perfect: the word of the Lord is tried: he is a buckler to all those that trust in him. For who is God save the Lord? Or who is a rock save our God? It is God that girdeth me with strength, and maketh my way perfect. He maketh my feet like hinds' feet, and setteth me upon my high places. (Ps. 18:29–33 KJV)

For by You I can run through a troop, and by my God I can leap over a wall. As for God, His way is perfect! The word of the Lord is tested and tried; He is a shield to all those who take refuge and put their trust in Him. For who is God except the Lord? Or who is the Rock save our God, The God who girds me with strength and makes my way perfect? He makes my feet like hinds' feet [able to stand firmly or make progress on the dangerous heights of testing and trouble]; He sets me securely upon my high places. (Ps. 18:29–33 AMP)

Again I rejoiced and thanked God for His awesome power and His unfailing love for me—the love that again showed the Devil whose child I was and that he was going over his boundary when he tried to bring fear and death upon me. I have a Father who is so jealous of me. He got angry when the Evil One tried to attack me and therefore stopped him in his tracks. Hallelujah! Glory to God!

The omnipotent One lifted me out of my bed, placed me on my feet to stand, and held me with His powerful hands. That was His way of telling the Devil, "Take your hands off My child—My property!" Oh how I love my Father. He is so sweet and so precious. God is amazing, is more than miraculous, and is simply marvelous.

> O give thanks unto the Lord; call upon his name: make known his deeds among the people. Sing unto him, sing psalms unto him: talk ye of all his wondrous works. Glory ye in his holy name: let the heart of them rejoice that seek the Lord. Seek the Lord, and his strength: seek his face evermore. Remember his marvelous works that he hath done; his wonders, and the judgments of his mouth. ... He suffered no man to do them wrong: yea, he reproved kings for their sakes; Saying, Touch not mine anointed, and do my prophets no harm. (Ps. 105:1–5, 14–15 KJV)

> O give thanks unto the Lord, call upon His name, make known His doings among the peoples! Sing to Him, sing praises to Him;

meditate on and talk of all His marvelous deeds and devoutly praise them. Glory in His holy name; let the hearts of those rejoice who seek and require the Lord [as their indispensable necessity]. Seek, inquire of and for the Lord, and crave Him and His strength (His might and inflexibility to temptation); seek and require His face and His presence [continually] evermore. [Earnestly] remember the marvelous deeds that He has done, His miracles and wonders, the judgments and sentences which He pronounced [upon His enemies, as in Egypt]. ... He allowed no man to do them wrong; in fact, He reproved kings for their sakes, Saying, Touch not My anointed, and do My prophets no harm. (Ps. 105:1–5, 14–15 AMP)

Chapter

Whatever He Says to You, Do It

God is not only concerned about the spiritual aspect of our lives but also the physical. He aims for us to be built up holistically, for the whole man (mind, body, and spirit) to be nurtured by His Word. Just spending time with Him, listening to His still, calm voice, and obeying Him can make a big difference in our lives.

One day as my husband and I entered the Vitamin Shoppe to purchase some vitamins, I heard the voice of the Lord telling me to buy prenatal vitamins.

"Prenatal?" I asked.

"Yes," He replied. "Use it daily along with your iron tablets to bring up your blood count."

Now, this was an answer to prayer because my blood count had been low for months, and though I tried taking everything with iron that I knew, nothing seemed to help. So I listened to the Lord's voice and purchased the prenatal tablets. Just a few weeks after using the tablets, I felt a difference in my body. I was not as weak and cold as I would normally be. After a month or so, I had more blood work done and was informed that my blood count was up. God did it again.

Some weeks later, after having the urge to take all meats out of my diet, I became a vegetarian for an entire year. I increased my daily intake of beans, raw vegetables, and fresh fruits. The Lord gave me ideas about putting different fresh fruits and raw vegetables together and making them into a juice. This brought about a remarkable change in my body, as my energy level increased and the swelling in my joints decreased. After one year of eating no meat, I then added wild salmon, chicken, and turkey to my diet. At that time I began to take note of all the things I ate and how they affected my body. I observed that after drinking cow's milk or milkshakes or consuming ice cream or anything sweet, the pains in my joints would increase, along with the swelling. So I started drinking soy milk instead of cow's milk and abstained from using sugar or any foods with large amounts of sugar. This resulted in a significant decrease of the pain and swelling in my joints.

About sixteen months after the diagnosis, the Lord spoke to me and told me to move my family to Richmond, Virginia. When my husband and I decided to move, my brother Joseph and wife made their house in Richmond available for us to rent, without a deposit or security and allowed us to pay the rent as it became available. For this we gave God thanks. When God told me to move, He also instructed me not to disclose this information to anyone until we completed the move. By now you would think that after all that God had brought me through, I would have been wise enough to do as He instructed. However, I went against what God said and convinced myself that it would be rude if I did not inform certain people of my move. So I did, and as you know, with every act of disobedience there are consequences—the consequences no one appreciates. Shortly after my disobedience, there was a decline in my health; I got worse physically. I was so sick I could not travel. My older sister, Yvonne, whom the Lord had appointed to help me move, also got terribly sick on the day we were scheduled to move. She found it very strange and went to seek the Lord in prayer. I knew it was because of my disobedience. I told my sister what I did by going against God's instruction and repented. God in His grace and mercy fixed it. I got better and was able to travel, and my sister's health was restored.

I learned a valuable lesson from this incident: I must trust God regardless of the circumstance. I was reminded that God sees and knows things we are unable to see or know. Therefore, He wants us to trust Him at His word. We do not need to know the reason why God tells us to do something. We just need to do as He says. He may not always tell us why, but nevertheless He wants us to trust Him.

In spite of my disobedience, God was still merciful and later told me why. He said, "The sickness came upon you from the Enemy through witchcraft, and the less the Enemy knew of your plans, the better it was for you. When you spoke your plans, he sent out his demons to prevent you from leaving. His aim was to kill you in New York. There was a spirit of envy and jealousy against you and your husband's marriage, and the Enemy wanted you dead."

As I said, I repented and asked God to help me maintain the spirit of total and complete obedience— obedience that would allow me to trust Him rather than question Him and that would help me to do what He says and when He says to do it, at all times.

Following this, my sister accompanied me and my children to Virginia. She told me that the Lord sent her there to be with us as our covering until my husband was able to join us. (He was believing God to receive a job in Virginia before permanently leaving his job in New York.) She also said she believed that within six months, my husband would be permanently there to stay.

My sister Yvonne was such a blessing. She was an anointed woman of God and an intercessor. She ministered to my children spiritually and physically. She helped them settle into their new surroundings (school, church, and neighborhood). She also helped them with their school work and taught them to do chores. It was so amazing how God used her to minister to us in every area.

During the time that God told her to come be with me and my children, she was the pastor of a small church in New York. She was with us Monday to Friday while she would minister to her congregants on the phone with the help of assistant pastors and leaders in New York. She drove to New York every Friday evening and returned to Virginia on Sunday evening. I knew this was hard for my sister, but she did it faithfully and lovingly, because when God gives you an assignment, He gives you the wisdom, strength, and grace to accomplish it.

I recall waking up in the middle of the night or in the wee hours of the morning, hearing my sister praying and interceding on behalf of me and family. She would declare healing as she also called forth the promises of God on our lives.

After work on Fridays my husband would come to Virginia and return to New York on Sunday nights. As my sister said, my husband came to be with us permanently within six months, and she returned to New York to do what God called her to do. Not only was my sister a prayer warrior and an intercessor, but she was also used mightily in the prophetic ministry.

Everything she said of my life and that of my family's, came to pass. One was, "Lois, I see you teaching at the school of Faith Landmarks Ministries when you are healed." I listened to her and laughed. I tried to accept what she said, but at the back of my mind I was wondering when this would happen. You see, many years had passed since my diagnosis of lupus, and I thought I would be completely healed by now. Therefore upon hearing this, I laughed, saying to myself, *When will this be?*

For we wrestle not against flesh and blood, but against principalities, against powers, against the rulers of the darkness of this world, against spiritual wickedness in high places. (Eph. 6:12 KJV)

For we are not wrestling with flesh and blood [contending only with physical opponents], but against the despotisms, against the powers, against [the master spirits who are] the world rulers of this present darkness, against the spirit forces of wickedness in the heavenly (supernatural) sphere. (Eph. 6:12 AMP)

And whatsoever we ask, we will receive of him, because we keep his commandments, and do those things that are pleasing in his sight. (1 John 3:22 KJV)

And we receive from Him whatever we ask, because we [[a]watchfully] obey His orders [observe His suggestions and injunctions, follow His plan for us] and [[b]habitually] practice what is pleasing to Him. (1 John 3:22 AMP)

Chapter

8

Help Is on the Way

One night, before my husband permanently moved to Virginia, my eldest son, Shane, said to me, "Mom, I will sleep with you in your bed tonight." I said okay and later realized that it was God who directed him to be there with me. Shortly after I fell asleep that night, I was awakened by severe pain and shortness of breath. The pain was very intense, and it was so hard to breathe. I felt as though I was about to faint, so I cried out to God for help. My son, who was alert at the time, was also praying and was able to help me get off the bed to go to the bathroom. I returned to my bed still fighting and praying, saying to my Father, "God, please send help." After much struggle and confession of the Word I eventually fell asleep early in the morning.

At about six o'clock in the morning, I received a phone call from a sister in Christ named Monica. As a member of Faith Landmarks Ministries, she volunteered in the Visitor's Department, greeting the new visitors of the church and praying for them as requested. A few days after my first visit at Faith Landmarks Ministries, Monica called to inform me that she read my prayer request that I wrote on the visitor's card to be healed of lupus. She prayed with me, encouraged me with the Word of God, and offered to help in any way she could that would make my life easier. She also informed me that she was a nurse and had some knowledge of what lupus entailed. This wonderful sister faithfully called me two or more times a week to pray and encourage me in the Word of God; she was a great blessing.

Her phone call that early morning, was to inform me that Rev. Hagin would be holding services that week at church. She asked if I would like to attend that morning service and offered to personally provide transportation. Immediately, I knew that this was an answer to my prayer for help, so I told her I would love to attend church. A few hours later Monica and her brother came to take me to church. I could not walk independently, so

Monica and her brother each held me by the arm, one on each side, took me to her car, and helped me walk into the church.

After praise and worship, Rev. Hagin went up to preach, but before he brought the Word he said, "We will spend some time in prayer. You can come to the altar, or you can stay in your seat." I stayed in my seat but decided to kneel. Though it took all the strength in me to get down on my knees, and in spite of all the pain it caused, I felt it was necessary. I was there for fifteen to twenty minutes praying and thanking God for my healing and His goodness, when all of a sudden I felt such an anointing. The rich presence of God was evident. When Rev. Hagin ended the prayer session, I got up a new person. I felt as if seventy-five percent of the pain had left my body; I felt good. The message by Rev. Hagin was powerful. I must confess I did not hear all of it because I was rejoicing in my healing. I could not wait to get home to share the news with my sister Yvonne and family.

At the completion of the service, Monica and her brother were both surprised at the miraculous power of God. Though experiencing some pain, I was still able to slowly walk and get into the car without any help. They all rejoiced with me at the touch of the master's hand on my life. Yes, God, my loving Father and my healer, did it. However, even though I knew this was a step toward my complete healing, I felt that there was something still holding me back.

The following Sunday my pastor preached on forgiveness. He said that if you believe you have forgiven someone, yet at the mention of the person's name or at the moment you see him or her you become angered, then you truly haven't forgiven him or her. At that moment I then remembered how two former friends wronged my husband: one lied about him, and the other stole from him. The lie prevented my husband from being hired for a new job that he was once promised. The money that this person stole was taken at a very inconvenient time. Not only was I sick and my husband the only source of income, but it was taken during the Christmas season. This limited the gifts that we were able to give to our children. For a while I was angry with these individuals, struggling to forgive them. At one point I did say I had forgiven them, but after hearing this sermon I realized I still had some resentment toward them. That day I prayed and asked the Lord to forgive me for not forgiving these individuals and to give me the strength to completely forgive them. I was free from holding on to such a heavy burden. It was my unforgiveness that was hampering my complete healing.

I then invested in healing cassettes of Rev. Hagin, Benny Hinn, and my pastor, Randy Gilbert. I played them 24–7, along with songs that professed healing, while also confessing God's Word over my body:

> My body is the temple of the living God. Therefore, spirit of infirmity, you have no access or control over my body. I rebuke all symptoms of lupus. I was and am healed by Jesus' stripes. In the name of Jesus, Satan, I command you to take your hands off my body. You have no authority, and therefore your attacks are ineffective. I am covered and healed by the blood of Jesus; I am whole.

While I was confessing the Word, the Lord instructed me to take communion daily for my healing. He said, "Take this along with My Word daily. This is My medication, and it has no side effects."

Is God not awesome? Now, that was an eye-opener for me. I began taking communion three times a day, at breakfast, lunch, and dinner, along with my daily medications and vitamins. I also anointed my body with olive oil, and I truly began to notice a difference in my body.

I then decided to go into prayer and fasting. Now, when it comes to praying and fasting, one cannot decide upon one's own will to give up food. For as humans, within our own flesh we are weak. We must know that God is directing us to do so, and in His strength He will allow us to walk through this sacrifice. Also when fasting, we must be expectant. We are not only strengthening our relationship with God but are also opening ourselves up to receive His blessings and promises over our lives. I was expecting God to work through me and in me to strengthen me physically but also to restore my confidence in Him.

Having confessed the Word, changed my diet, taken daily communion, and anointed myself with olive oil, I knew that now I needed to do as I had declared. I decided that I needed to step out in faith and dance before the Lord, praising Him with my whole being. Therefore, I began dancing in my living room. In pain, I stood against the wall and lifted my feet one at a time, saying, "Feet, you will praise God; you will dance. In the name of Jesus, you will dance." I did this repeatedly as I moved and danced to the music. Then, while bracing against the wall to support my body, I took one hand, used it to lift the other, and said, "Hands, you will praise God."

I did this daily for a period of time. Alternating my hands and feet, I continued to command them to praise God, sometimes with tears rolling down my cheeks because of the excruciating, unbearable pain. After a while, my joints got stronger, the pain lessened, and the strength in my entire body increased.

Then one day, something incredible happened. Deeply engaged into worship, as I was entering into God's presence, I felt an anointed spirit in the room. I looked around and saw no one, so I continued dancing. At this point I was so engrossed in my praise and worship that I no longer needed to use the wall for support. As I was on my feet dancing, I began to move more freely. Then I heard a sound—a sound that was very puzzling at first. Again I looked around, still not seeing anyone or anything. The sound, which I now recognized as the flapping of wings, began to get louder and louder. This flapping of wings was melodic, as it was in rhythm with the music. Then it dawned on me—angels! Angels were dancing with me!

"My God," I said, "You are awesome!" This was an unbelievable moment. It's a moment I enjoyed and have cherished secretly for years, fearing the disbelief of others. Regardless, I know it was real.

The presence of the Lord was in my living room, and His angels were dancing with me. As I danced I felt such love from my heavenly Father. Such joy came over me that as I danced and danced, I began to laugh. I was overtaken with laughter to the point that I became drunk in the Spirit. Intoxicated, I fell prostrate on my living room floor as the Lord ministered to me. An hour or so later when I got up, I felt free. God delivered me and strengthened me, giving me the ability to freely dance before Him. It was and still is awesome.

I began doing house work again, praising God every step of the way. I also joined the women's basketball team at Faith Landmarks Ministries. This was a big victory for my son, Joel, because his prayer was answered. I was able to play basketball with him again. You should have seen the smile on his face when I walked onto the court and challenged him; it was great. I can imagine God laughing and saying to the Devil, "Do you see My daughter Lois? She is playing basketball."

God is our refuge and strength, a very pleasant help in trouble. (Ps. 46:1 KJV)

God is our Refuge and Strength [mighty and impenetrable to temptation], a very present and well-proved help in trouble. (Ps. 46:1 AMP)

Our soul waiteth for the Lord: he is our help and our shield. (Ps. 33:20 KJV)

Our inner selves wait [earnestly] for the Lord; He is our Help and our Shield. (Ps. 33:20 AMP)

Chapter

It's Your Time!

Sometime later, when my medication got low, I placed a request for a refill on the two medications: Plaquinell and Celebrex. Due to a snowstorm that lasted for more than a week, I was unable to pick up my refills, which resulted in me being off my medication for quite some time. Though Plaquenill and Celebrex were used for the lupus and arthritis, I realized after being off these medications for over a week that I was feeling great. This was when I knew that I was completely healed. Therefore, I never returned to pick up the medication.

Four months later, I visited my doctor for a checkup and blood work. He asked if I was keeping up with the daily dosage of the medications. I said, "No, I have not used them for four months and two weeks. I do not need them because I am healed. I am doing well, with no pain."

His response was, "You are in remission. Keep using the medications."

He then scheduled me to see him in six months. I returned six months later to see him and was asked the same question again about my medication usage. My response again was, "No I do not need them, for I am healed."

He looked at me very annoyed and said, "No one has ever been healed of lupus."

I looked him in the eye and said, "Well, you are looking at a woman who has been healed of lupus. I know I am healed; there were things that I could not do before that I am doing now. Do you believe in the power of prayer?"

He bent his head, walked away, and then stopped and said, "Promise me you will continue to use the Plaquenill; it is good for high cholesterol."

I simply responded saying, "No I am not taking it. I do not have high cholesterol."

Also, in the back of my mind I knew that this drug was not even aimed at controlling levels of cholesterol. Having never mentioned anything about cholesterol, he just wanted me to stay on the medication. I could see that the Devil was mad that I was healed. He had messed with God's property for long enough.

Anyone who saw me before knew there was a transformation. A month before that last doctor's visit that I just mentioned, my family and I went to Universal Studios in Orlando, Florida, where my healing was made evident. The Hulk rollercoaster, recently added to the park, is a ride that is known for its speed, long drops, and quick turns. I got on the Hulk rollercoaster and came off feeling well and rejoicing in the Lord for His healing power. Now, you tell me: was that not a transformation? From lying in my bed in pain, weak and nauseated, and incapable of helping myself, to going on the Hulk rollercoaster and completing the ride without any pain or without experiencing any of my past symptoms like dizziness—this indeed was the supernatural work of God. I can just imagine God looking down and having a *big laugh* at the Devil.

Some months later I started working at Victory Christian Academy (my church's school) as a supervisor in the after-school program. Two years later I began working in the school as an assistant kindergarten teacher. The first day as I walked into the building to my assigned class, I remembered the words my sister

Yvonne prophesied over me: "I see you working as a teacher at the school of Faith Landmarks Ministries." I laughed a laugh of thanksgiving and a laugh at the Devil because there I was indeed, teaching.

I am now proud to say that after some years of teaching, I have been a small business owner in the fields of catering and gift basket making. I have also worked eight to twelve hours a day with physically and mentally challenged adults. This is nothing but the miraculous power of God. God is alive and still heals. The fact that I once was bedridden, unable to hold a pen or a toothbrush, and had to be carried by my husband as if I was a baby, yet now I am on my feet for over twelve hours, able to lift more than twenty pounds and care for individuals who are helpless, just shows you the power of prayer, confession, and faith. Yes, this may not be the case for all lupus patients. Nevertheless I thank God for allowing my life to be a testimony of His healing power.

Now when the Devil tries to approach me with his foolishness, I remind him of the stripes Jesus took on His back two thousand years ago for my healing. *I serve him the back of Jesus.* Whenever the Enemy tries to attack you or your family, I also encourage you to serve him the back of Jesus. Tell him to *look at the back of Jesus.*

I will sing unto the Lord, for he hath triumphed gloriously: the horse and his rider hath he thrown into the sea. The Lord is my strength and song, and he is become my salvation. (Exod. 15:1–2 KJV)

I will sing to the Lord, for He has triumphed gloriously; the horse and his rider or its chariot has He thrown into the sea. The Lord is my Strength and my Song, and He has become my Salvation. (Exod. 15:1–2 AMP)

Many are the afflictions of the righteous: but the Lord delivereth him out of them all. He keepeth all his bones: not one of them is broken. (Ps. 34:19–20 KJV)

Many evils confront the [consistently] righteous, but the Lord delivers him out of them all. He keeps all his bones; not one of them is broken. (Ps. 34:19–20 AMP)

Chapter

The Back of Jesus

As I look at the back of Jesus, I begin to think of my back—the back of a human being. What is the purpose of the back? Why do we need it? Can we survive without it? The back—rising from the top of the buttocks to the back of the neck and shoulders—is the rear part of the human body that serves to support and protect. The back provides support for the head and trunk of the body, regulating strength, flexibility, and overall movement. Supported by the ribcage and shoulders, the spine provides nerves to the rest of the body. So, what would happen if I had no back? How would my body be supported if I were to crucially injure my back? How would my body be protected? At worst, there would be a lack of support and structure and an inability to stand. The bottom line is, without a back, one is unable to be productive. Depending on the situation, one may not even be able to survive.

Now, if the back is that important to the human body, then how much more important is the back of Jesus to the body of Christ? As the body of Christ, Jesus is our foundation, our support, and our strength. So even as the human back serves to support and protect the body, so does the blood-striped back of Jesus support and protect the body of Christ. What Jesus endured on His back serves as the foundation for His believers. Due to God sacrificing His Son, Jesus, who obediently took the stripes on His back and was crucified on the cross, shedding His blood for the forgiveness of our sins, we the body are entitled to healing, protection, support, and eternal life with God in heaven. Without Jesus' sacrifice, there would be no salvation available for man. The relationship of man to God would have remained unrestored, disunited; there would be a spiritual void.

Jesus was betrayed by His own, arrested, and placed through a long trial. After being judged and condemned, He was mocked, scorned, taunted, spat upon, and whipped many times. He was then given a cross to carry on His back for miles. With blood saturating His back, He was left with torn flesh. Still Jesus had to bear this cross.

I cannot begin to imagine the pain and agony He went through as He carried the cross on His back. And when I think of it all, my Jesus did it for me, and you— yes, He did it for you. Jesus took those stripes for our healing, and He shed His blood for the forgiveness of our sins. Therefore *His back supports and protects us.* It supports us in times of trouble, at times when we feel all alone and there is no human help or support.

At times you may feel as though you have no earthly support. This can especially be experienced in the life of a single parent. Sometimes you are left alone to train, discipline, to overall provide for the needs of your family. Even for parents in general, there are times where no matter how well you train your children, the Devil will continue to tempt them. You may have taught them the ways of God and brought them up in the house of God, but still somehow they manage to go astray. Now people who you have depended on for years are now pulling away because of the stigma attached to your present situation.

You begin to ask God, "Why? Why my child? Why me? Why my family?" Then you begin to find blame in everyone and everything. You point fingers at each other as parents, as husband and wife, or you blame yourself as a father or mother. If only you had done this or hadn't done that; if only his father was here or his mother. Then the Enemy continues to bring condemnation, guilt, depression, strife, separation, shame, and sometimes sickness.

However, Jesus is with you. He is saying, "I am your support! Though you may have made some mistakes as an individual, as a parent, or as a spouse you do not have to suffer from the consequences of your faults. That is why I went to the cross; that is why I took the whips on My back and shed My blood. I shed My blood so you can be set free of all condemnation and pain. By accepting Me into your life, asking Me for forgiveness, and making Me Lord over your life, you become a part of My body. I, the Lord Jesus Christ, become your covering. I will look out for you and protect you because I am here to set you free. So do not be dismayed and do not give up. I will strengthen you. I am with you. *Look at My back.* I am your protector, and I am your support."

> Fear thou not; for I am with thee: be
> not dismayed for I am thy God: I will
> strengthen thee; yea, I will help thee; yea,

I will uphold thee with the right hand of
my righteousness. (Isa. 41:10 KJV)

"I am always holding you together—your body,
your children, your spouse, and your entire family. I
am supporting you; I am protecting you. I have got you
covered, as *you are covered by My blood—the blood of
Jesus.* I am here to set you free. My blood was shed
to forgive you of your sins and to also make whole
everything in your life that is broken. Everything
that is out of place has to come in line because of My
shed blood.

"So when the storms of life come and when the
Enemy comes to torment you, look at My back. When
he tells you that you will not make it or that it is over,
look at My back. Remember what I did for you and
serve him *the back of Jesus*! Say to him, 'Satan, *I serve
you the back of Jesus. Look at the back of Jesus!* I am
forgiven, supported, protected, covered, and healed by
the stripes on His back and the blood He shed for me two
thousand years ago. I am covered by the *blood of Jesus,*
and therefore, all of your lies, threats, and schemes are
over. They are ended in the name of Jesus.'

"Then go rejoice! Look at all the blessings in your
life, and *praise* Me. As you praise Me in the midst of

your darkness, you will get the victory. *Praise Me, laugh in the face of the Enemy, and dance before Me.* Like the walls of Jericho fell when the children of Israel obeyed instruction, even so will those walls in your life and the lives of your children and loved ones. The walls the Enemy has placed in your family's life will fall when you *praise* Me. I am your God and your Savior, your support, protector, and healer, and I want and have the best for you. *Rejoice* and *laugh* at the Enemy, and speak to your situation. Speak My *Word* and watch Me work. Life and death are in the power of the tongue. Therefore it is important that you pay close attention to the things you allow to come out of your mouth. Therefore, do not speak what you see, but speak *My* Word. Say what I say and speak My promises, for My Word is life and brings health to the body."

As a survivor, I encourage you to start speaking God's Word to the dead and unhealthy things in your life. Expect a transformation, and watch as they come alive. Try speaking the following confessions and declarations daily. Do it audibly, and make it personal by saying your name, the names of family members or individuals that you are praying for, along with other Bible verses that relate to your situation. Search the Word. Look for Bible verses that relate to your situation, and pray those verses. The Word of God said decree a thing and it shall come to pass. "Thou shalt also decree a thing, and it shall be established unto thee: and the light shall shine upon thy ways" (Job 22:28 KJV). Confess them daily, and see God change and transform the situations in your life. God's Word is *powerful! Let it work for you!*

Daily Declarations

I decree and declare the following:

> As the hart panteth after the water brooks, so panteth [say name of individual] soul after thee, O God. (Ps. 42:1 KJV)

> As the hart pants and longs for the water brooks, so [say name of individual] pant and long for you O God. (Ps. 42:1 AMP)

> The spirit of the Lord will rest upon, [say name of individual], the spirit of wisdom and understanding, the spirit of counsel and might, the spirit of knowledge and

of the fear of the Lord: And shall make him of quick understanding in the fear of the Lord: and he shall not judge after the sight of his eyes, neither reprove after the hearing of his ears. (Isa. 11:2–3 KJV)

And the Spirit of the Lord shall rest upon, [say name of individual], the Spirit of wisdom and understanding, the Spirit of counsel and might, the Spirit of knowledge and of the reverential and obedient fear of the Lord—And shall make him of quick understanding, and his delight shall be in the reverential and obedient fear of the Lord. And he shall not judge by the sight of his eyes, neither decide by the hearing of his ears. (Isa. 11:2–3 AMP)

And all thy children will be taught of the Lord; and great shall be the peace of thy children. (Isa. 54:13 KJV)

And all your [spiritual] children shall be disciples [taught by the Lord and obedient to His will], and great shall be the peace and undisturbed composure of your children. (Isa. 54:13 AMP)

For he hath made him to be sin for us, who knew no sin; that we might be made the righteousness of God in him. (2 Cor. 5:21 KJV)

For our sake He made Christ [virtually] to be sin Who knew no sin, so that in and through Him we might become [[a]endued with, viewed as being in, and examples of] the righteousness of God [what we ought to be, approved and acceptable and in right relationship with Him, by His goodness]. (2 Cor. 5:21 AMP)

And the Lord shall make thee the head, and not the tail; and thou shalt be above only, and thou shalt not be beneath. (Deut. 28:13 KJV)

And the Lord shall make you the head, and not the tail; and you shall be above only, and you shall not be beneath. (Deut. 28:13 AMP)

Greater is He that is in you than he that is in the world. (1 John 4. 4b KJV)

He Who lives in you is greater (mightier) than he who is in the world. (1 John 4:4b AMP)

I can do all things through Christ who strengtheneth me. (Phil. 4:13 KJV)

I have strength for all things in Christ
Who empowers me [I am ready for
anything and equal to anything through
Him Who infuses inner strength into me;
I am self-sufficient in Christ's sufficiency].
(Phil. 4:13 AMP)

God is my strength and power: and
he maketh my way perfect. (2 Sam.
22:33 KJV)

God is my strong Fortress; He guides the
blameless in His way and sets him free. (2
Sam. 22:33 AMP)

For God hath not given us the spirit of
fear; but of power, and of love, and of a
sound mind. (2 Tim. 1:7 KJV)

For God did not give us a spirit of timidity
(of cowardice, of craven and cringing and

fawning fear), but [He has given us a spirit] of power and of love and of calm and well-balanced mind and discipline and self-control. (2 Tim. 1:7 AMP)

We have the mind of Christ. (1 Cor. 2:16b KJV)

We have the mind of Christ (the Messiah) and do hold the thoughts (feelings and purposes) of His heart. (1 Cor. 2:16b AMP)

What? know ye not that your body is the temple of the Holy Ghost which is in you, which ye have of God, and ye are not your own? (1 Cor. 6:19 KJV)

Do you not know that your body is the temple (the very sanctuary) of the Holy Spirit Who lives within you, Whom you have received [as a Gift] from God? You are not your own). (1 Cor. 6:19 AMP)

Surely goodness and mercy shall follow me all the days of my life: and I will dwell in the house of the Lord for ever. (Ps. 23:6 KJV)

Surely or only goodness, mercy, and unfailing love shall follow me all the days of my life, and through the length of my days the house of the Lord [and His presence] shall be my dwelling place. (Ps. 23:6 AMP)

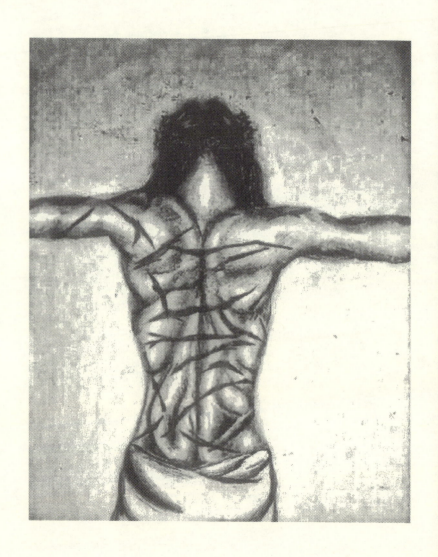

What Does the Back of Jesus Mean to Me?

B: Broken Body Heals My Brokenness
"This is my body, which is broken for you: this do in remembrance of me" (1 Cor. 11:24 KJV).When I look at Jesus' back, I am reminded of the stripes He took. As He allowed His body to be torn and broken, He was taking care of all the brokenness in my life. Therefore, anything in my life, whether it is physical, emotional, or psychological, that is not working in the manner in which God designed for it to work, I decree and declare it to be mended. In the name of Jesus, all the broken things in my life are made whole. Jesus paid it all.

A: Always Present
"So I will be with thee: I will not fail thee, nor forsake thee" (Josh. 1:5b KJV). Even as God promised this to Joshua, God also gives us this same promise. Throughout

my battle with lupus and arthritis, I have held on to His words. I knew that in spite of the tremendous pain that I was enduring, or regardless of the emotional distress I was facing, God was still by my side. The stripes on His Son's back were a constant reminder of the healing that was to come, and His eternal presence helped comfort and encourage me as I held on to His Word.

C: Christ Became a Curse for Me

"Christ hath redeemed us from the curse of the law, being made a curse for us ... That the blessing of Abraham might come on the Gentiles through Jesus Christ; that we might receive the promise of the Spirit through faith" (Gal. 3:13a–14 KJV). Because of Christ's redemptive power, I am free from the curse of sin and from all curses. I boldly confess that in the name of Jesus and by the blood of the Lamb, all ancestral and generational curses are broken from my life and that of my family's. They are cut off from our lives, not to return or become reactivated. I look at Jesus' back and know that through His death, He removed all curses, replacing them with blessings: Sickness was replaced with health, poverty with wealth, fear with faith, shame with honor, and sorrow with joy. I will continue to walk in the abundant blessings of God.

K: Keeps Me Focused on Him

As I look at the back of Jesus, I remember what He did for me on the cross and what He continues to do for me today. The constant reminder of Him saving me and healing me of lupus and rheumatoid arthritis keeps me focused on Him and His Word. It empowers me to live a victorious life.

J: Justice Was Served

"Therefore, since we are now justified (acquitted, made righteous, and brought into right relationship with God) by Christ's blood, how much more [certain is it that] we shall be saved by Him from the indignation and wrath of God" (Rom. 5:9 AMP). By the shedding of His blood, I have been made justified. The guilt and penalty of my sins were removed from me when Jesus endured the whips on His back. Through His sacrificial death on the cross, the shedding of His blood declared me free and righteous.

E: Eternal Life

"For the wages of sin is death; but the gift of God is eternal life through Jesus Christ our Lord" (Rom. 6:23 KJV). After being forgiven of my sins, I am now called righteous. I look forward to enjoying the gift of eternal life with my Savior.

S: Salvation Is Mine

"But God, who is rich in mercy, for his great love wherewith he loved us, Even when we were dead in sins, hath quickened us together with Christ, (by grace ye are saved;) And hath raised us up together, and made us sit together in heavenly places in Christ Jesus" (Eph. 2:4–6 KJV). By the shedding of His blood, I am delivered from sin and its consequences and will reign with Him in heaven.

U: Unfailing, Unconditional Love

"But God shows and clearly proves His [own] love for us, by the fact that while we were still sinners, Christ (the Messiah, the Anointed One) died for us" (Rom. 5:8 AMP). "Herein is love, not that we loved God, but that he loved us, and sent his Son to be the propitiation for our sins" (1 John 4:10 AMP). Jesus loves me regardless of who I am or what I have done. With no concern for Himself or His persona, desires, or wants, He went to the cross for me. "Greater love hath no man than this, that a man lay down his life for his friends" (John 15:13 KJV).

S: Strength and Supernatural Power

"It is God that girdeth me with strength, and maketh my way perfect. He maketh my feet like hinds' feet, and setteth me upon my high places. He teacheth my hands to war, so that a bow of steel is broken by mine arms" (Ps. 18:32–34 KJV). Jesus Christ gives me strength and supernatural power to fight against all the darts of the Enemy, which includes all sicknesses, diseases, poverty, and areas of lack.

As the Church/the Body of Christ, What Should the Back of Jesus Mean to Us?

"For by one Spirit are we all baptized into one body, whether we be Jews or Gentiles, whether we be bond or free; and have been all made to drink into one Spirit" (1 Cor. 12:13 KJV). When we ask Jesus to forgive us of our sins and invite Him into our lives, we become a part of His body—the church; we are born-again believers. He then becomes our support and our protector, as His Word says that He will never leave us or forsake us (Josh. 1:5b KJV).

Jesus will always be our source of strength and our wing of protection throughout any situation that may arise in our lives: "When thou passest through the waters, I will be with thee; and through the rivers, they shall not overflow thee: when thou walkest through the fire, thou shalt not be burned; neither shall the flame kindle upon thee" (Isa. 43:2 KJV).

B: Basis of Our Faith

"And he is the head of the body, the church: who is the beginning, the firstborn from the dead; that in all things he might have the preeminence" (Col. 1:18 KJV). Jesus Christ is the head of the church and should be in control at all times; He must take first place.

A: Atonement

"Who his own self bare our sins in his own body on the tree, that we, being dead to sins, should live unto righteousness" (1 Pet. 2:24). God's relationship with man was broken when Adam and Eve sinned. Through their disobedience, not only did it break the covenant but it also resulted in the separation of God and mankind. However, God, through His love, mercy, and compassion, has restored our relationship with Him. This He did through the sacrificial death of His Son Jesus Christ.

To complete this reconciliation, man was left to do his part: "All we like sheep have gone astray; we have turned everyone to his own way; and the Lord hath laid on him the iniquity of us all" (Isa. 53:6 KJV). First, we are to acknowledge our mistakes and accept His gift of salvation. Then we ask for God's forgiveness, which will then make us His sons and daughters. As His children, which He calls the church or the body of Christ, as we spend time developing our relationship with God, living a life that glorifies Him, the Lord begins to pour out His anointing on us. This anointing strengthens the church, enabling His children to live a victorious life and to do the work God has called them to do. Therefore through the *atonement,* we are *anointed* and *appointed* to do the work of God.

C: Chosen Ones

"But ye are a chosen generation, a royal priesthood, an holy nation, a peculiar people; that we should shew forth the praises of him who hath called you out of darkness into his marvelous light" (1 Pet. 2:9 KJV). Jesus, having completed His purpose on earth, by making it possible for us to repent of our sins and receive Him as Lord of our lives, united us with our heavenly Father. After being called out and chosen by God, the church was then given a commission: "Go ye into all the world and preach the gospel to every creature" (Mark 16:15 KJV). We are to go into every man's world and offer them the gift of salvation that God has given us.

K: Kingdom Minded

"But seek ye first the kingdom of God and his righteousness and all these things shall be added unto you" (Matt. 6:33 KJV). As we put God first, sacrificing our time, laying aside our desires, and following His will for our lives, God will in turn take care of all of our needs.

J: Justified

"Therefore being justified by faith, we have peace with God through our Lord Jesus Christ: By whom also we have access by faith into this grace wherein we stand, and rejoice in hope of the glory of God" (Rom. 5:1–2 KJV). To be justified means to be declared or made righteous in the sight of God. By Jesus shedding His blood, we are not only forgiven but we are also welcomed into His kingdom. We have the opportunity to be in right standing with God.

E: Eternal Life

"For the wages of sin is death; but the gift of God is eternal life through Jesus Christ our Lord" (Rom. 6:23 KJV). After accepting His gift (Jesus, His Son) and living a life of obedience, our ultimate promise is everlasting life with Him in heaven.

S: Salvation

"For by grace you have been saved through faith. And this is not your own doing; it is the gift of God: Not of works, lest any man should boast." (Eph. 2:8–9 KJV)

U: United with Christ

"There is one body, and one spirit, even as we are called in one hope of our calling." (Eph. 4:4 KJV) Having been reconciled, the church becomes one with God the Father, the Son, and the Holy Spirit. We operate in a spirit of unity so that we the church can accomplish God's will for His people on earth.

S: Salt of the Earth

"Ye are the salt of the earth: but if the salt have lost his savour, wherewith shall it be salted? It is thenceforth good for nothing, but to be cast out, and to be trodden under   foot of men. Ye are the light of the world. A city that is set on an hill cannot be hid. ...Let your light so shine before men, that they may see your good works, and glorify your Father which is in heaven." (Matt.5:13-14, 16 KJV)

As the body of Christ, we are the salt of the earth, meaning we should be leaving a positive impact wherever we go, always adding value to the lives of people. We are a representation of Christ and therefore must live and act according to His Word.

Likewise, as the body of Christ, as we share the Word of God with others, our speech should be seasoned with grace: "Let your speech be always with grace, seasoned with salt, that ye may know how ye ought to answer every man" (Col. 4:6 KJV). When we speak, the love of God should flow through us. Being the *salt* of the earth with renewed *speech*, Jesus now *sends* us out to the world with His *supernatural power* in effort to seek the lost and to lead them to Him—the Savior: "And Jesus came and spake unto them, saying, All power is given unto me in heaven and in earth. Go ye therefore, and teach all nations, baptizing them in the name of the Father, and of the Son, and of the Holy Ghost" (Matt 28:18–19 KJV). Jesus Christ has given us supernatural power to heal the sick, raise the dead, and cast out demons.

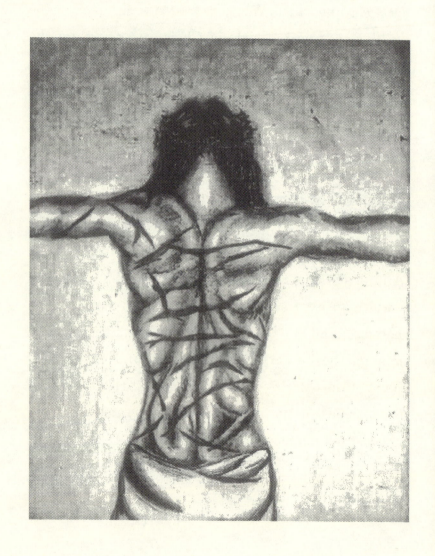

Having read my testimony and the significance of Jesus' crucifixion, what does the back of Jesus mean to you? Take some time to reflect, and for each of the following letters, fill in the acronym, answering the question, "What does the back of Jesus mean to me?"

The

B:

A:

C:

K:

Of

J:

E:

S:

U:

S:

Chapter

Miracles, Miracles, Miracles!

I thank God that now, twelve years later, I am still healed and will continue to walk in my healing by the grace of God. I am still interceding for others and giving God glory for all the things He has done in and through my life, my family's life, and the lives of others. There were so many miracles God performed after my sickness, and I simply cannot complete this book without mentioning a few.

After moving into the house in Virginia, we found out that it was not as comfortable as we initially thought. The house was built in 1948, and the windows were never changed or the insulation upgraded. There were also some parts of the house that were never insulated. Due to this, when it was hot, the house was difficult to cool and when cold difficult to warm. During the cold months, we would place one hundred gallons of oil in the boiler, and it would last for five to seven days, depending on how cold the days were. Because of this, it took a large amount of money to heat the house. Needless to say, we accumulated a huge credit card debt, and my husband, in disgust, said, "This is it; we are not using our credit card anymore to purchase oil. When the oil is done, we will use kerosene space heaters instead."

One day after having my quiet time with the Lord, I went downstairs to get some water. On my way to the kitchen, I had an urge to go to the boiler room. Walking over to the boiler and while placing my hand on it, I said, "Lord, let this boiler run until we get the money to purchase some oil." I left the boiler room and went on to get my water. The following week the boiler was still running, and the house felt much warmer than usual. I called it supernatural heat.

My husband asked me, "Lois, did you order oil?" I said no while laughing. He then said in a very stern voice, "Did I not say that we are not buying anymore oil?"

Pointing above, I repeated, "I did not, but our Father did."

My husband walked away upset, saying, "You must think this is a joke."

I laughed uncontrollably. The following, day my husband asked again if I ordered oil, and I told him that what was happening was a result of my prayer. My husband was stunned. I said to him, "God multiplied the oil." He was still in shock, and I must admit that at first I was walking around in a daze myself.

I shared this with family members and friends, indicating how surprised I was. Then one day the Lord said to me, "Why are you surprised? Why are you surprised that I multiplied the oil? This is who I am; I am the God of miracles. You should expect miracles at any time and should not be surprised when I perform them."

I said, "Yes, Lord, help my disbelief."

After three months of enjoying this miracle, one day the boiler stopped. I flipped the switch, but nothing happened. I said, "God, what are You doing to me? I have been boasting about You multiplying the oil, and now it has stopped."

Then the Lord said, "Tomorrow your husband is getting paid, and you will be able to purchase oil."

Right then and there, the Lord allowed me to hear myself. Actually, it was so realistic that it appeared as though He turned on a television screen. I was able to see myself with my hands on the boiler, saying, "Lord, let this boiler run until we get the money to purchase some oil." I told God what I wanted, and He gave me exactly that. That day I was reminded that *you possess what you confess, or in other words, you get what you ask for.* My God was so concerned about our well-being that He allowed the boiler to stop on a warm day, when we would not need any heat. This gave us enough time to order oil for the following day. It should also be noted, that during this three month period, we were able to pay the entire credit card bill.

A few years after my healing, while driving my daughter to school, I heard a loud sound coming from the left front tire of my van. I pulled over to check, and my daughter and I saw that we had a flat. I took my daughter to school and stopped at a gas station on my way home to put air in the tire. To my surprise, the air pump was out of order, so I headed home to get my two other children to take them to school.

I started praying, asking the Lord to take me home safely and to guide the van as I took my children to school. Then I continued praying in tongues. A block away from my house, the noise coming from the tire stopped, and the van began to run smoothly. When I pulled into my yard, I asked my son to check the tire. To my surprise, he said the tire was no longer flat. I exited the van to check the tire myself, and indeed, it was back to normal. Hallelujah! The Lord did it again! He fixed my tire while I drove. This tire kept going and lasted for a very long time.

I tell you: our God is more than amazing, more than marvelous, and more than miraculous. He is more than wonderful; a miracle-working God, He is the same yesterday, today, and forever. *Bless His holy name.*

> I will bless the Lord at all times; his praise shall continually be in my mouth. My soul shall make her boast in the Lord: the humble shall hear thereof and be glad. O magnify the Lord with me, and let us exalt his name together. I sought the Lord, and he heard me, and delivered me from all my fears. (Ps. 34:1–4 KJV)

> I will bless the Lord at all times; His praise shall continually be in my mouth. My life makes its boast in the Lord; let the humble and afflicted hear and be glad. O magnify the Lord with me, and let us exalt His name together. I sought (inquired of) the Lord and required Him [of necessity and on the authority of His Word], and He heard me, and delivered me from all my fears. (Ps. 34:1–4 AMP)

He that dwelleth in the secret place of the most High shall abide under the shadow of the Almighty. I will say of the Lord, He is my refuge and my fortress: my God in him will I trust. Surely he shall deliver thee from the snare of the fowler, and from the noisome pestilence. He shall cover thee with his feathers, and under his wings shall thou trust: his truth shall be thy shield and buckler. Thou shalt not be afraid for the terror by night; nor for the arrow that flieth by day; Nor for the pestilence that walketh in darkness; nor for the destruction that wasteth at noonday. A thousand shall fall at thy side, and ten thousand at thy right hand; but it shall not come nigh thee. Only with thine eyes shall thou behold and see the reward of the wicked. Because he hath made the Lord, which is my refuge, even the most High, thy habitation; There shall no evil befall thee, neither shall any plague come nigh thy dwelling. For he shall give his angels charge over thee, to keep thee in all thy ways. They shall bear thee up in their hands, lest thou dash thy foot against a stone. Thou shall tread upon the lion and adder: the young lion and the dragon shalt thou trample under feet. Because he hath set his love upon me, therefore will I deliver him: I will set him on high, because he hath known my name. He shall call upon me, and I will answer him: I will be with him in trouble; I will deliver him, and honor him. With long life will I satisfy him, and shew him my salvation. (Ps. 91 KJV)

He who dwells in the secret place of the Most High shall remain stable and fixed under the shadow of the Almighty [Whose power no foe can withstand]. I will say of the Lord, He is my Refuge and my Fortress, my God; on Him I lean and rely, and in Him I [confidently] trust! For [then] He will deliver you from the snare of the fowler and from the deadly pestilence. [Then] He will cover you with His pinions, and under His wings shall you trust and find refuge; His truth and His faithfulness are a shield and a buckler. You shall not be afraid of the terror of the night, nor of the arrow (the evil plots and slanders of the wicked) that flies by day, Nor of the pestilence that stalks in darkness, nor of the destruction and sudden death that surprise and lay waste at noonday. A thousand may fall at your side, and ten thousand at your right hand, but it shall not come near you. Only a spectator shall you be [yourself inaccessible in the secret place of the Most High] as you witness the reward of the wicked. Because you have made the Lord your refuge, and the Most High your dwelling place, There shall no evil befall you, nor any plague or calamity come near your tent. For He will give His angels [especial] charge over you to accompany and defend and preserve you in all your ways [of obedience and service]. They shall bear you up on their hands, lest you dash your foot against a stone. You shall tread upon the lion and adder; the young lion and the serpent shall you trample underfoot. Because he has set his love upon Me, therefore will I deliver him; I will set him on high, because he knows and understands My name [has a personal knowledge of My mercy, love, and kindness—trusts and relies on Me, knowing I will never forsake him, no, never]. He shall call upon Me, and I will answer him; I will be with him in trouble, I will deliver him and honor him. With long life will I satisfy him and show him My salvation. (Ps. 91 AMP)

Printed in the United States
By Bookmasters